The Munger House:
A History of Wichita's Oldest House

By:
Keith Wondra and James Vannurden

© Copyright 2020 by Keith Wondra and
James Vannurden

All Rights Reserved

ISBN: 978-1-929731-48-0

Contents

Acknowledgements — vii

Introduction — ix

1. Darius Munger — 1

2. Construction of the Munger House — 9

3. Munger's Occupation — 15

4. W. C. Woodman's Occupation — 21

5. Other Owners — 27

6. Munger House at Old Cowtown Museum — 37

7. Restorations — 49

Conclusion — 61

Bibliography — 63

Appendix — 67

Acknowledgements

Writing a book on a building that is integral to the history of Wichita, like the Munger House, could not be done without help from the community. Unless otherwise noted, all photographs presented here are from Old Cowtown Museum's collections. Old Cowtown Museum has undergone numerous name changes in its history. For the sake of consistency Old Cowtown Museum will be used throughout except for in direct quotations.

Even though Old Cowtown Museum has many pictures covering the Munger House's 150 years of existence other institutions and persons contributed photographs to complete the book including Nichole Conard of RedRock Photography, Jaime Green of *The Wichita Eagle*, Paul Oberg of the McCormick School Museum, Crystal Socha, and Keith Wondra.

Introduction

The story of the Munger House and its survival parallels that of the city of Wichita. Each sprang up in the middle of an unsettled wilderness and prospered. From the humble beginnings to the endurance through time, this house mirrors the city of Wichita itself, and its story lives on.

Darius Munger himself survived and thrived in a new town on the Great Plains. He took a risk building his home in an unsettled area. Munger performed many necessary jobs, including platting of the town. He became a welcoming host as a hotel owner to those who also dared to start anew in Wichita.

The construction of the house itself was a great ordeal. Building a two-story home alone was a daunting task. He procured the supplies himself and worked month after month with little civilization around him. Starting in the fall of 1868 and finishing in the spring of 1869, Munger's home was a great addition to the landscape of the area that would soon become Wichita.

The Munger House not only served as a dwelling for Darius, his wife, and their two daughters, but held multiple functions. The Munger House served as a hotel. Before those choosing to make Wichita their new home, settlers needed a place to stay. The house also served as a home away from home for travelers.

Munger also conducted city business within the walls of his home. He served as an early postmaster, with his kitchen serving as a post office. Munger also served as the justice of the peace while in the home. Church services were also held upstairs in the hotel from time to time.

When Munger sold his house in 1874, W.C. Woodman became the new owner. He was the president and founder of the First Arkansas Valley Bank. Woodman had the house remodeled and expanded. Its new name became Lakeside.

After the Woodman family, ownership of the house changed several times over the years. First, newspaperman P.J. Conklin owned the house. It was then purchased by Dr. and Mrs. Fuller, who had it for many years. Finally, the local chapter of the Daughters of the American Revolution purchased the home with the idea of restoring it to its former glory as the Munger House. They eventually decided to donate the house to the newly founded Historic Wichita, Inc. (later known as Historic Wichita Cow Town and now known as Old Cowtown Museum.)

For its last 67 years the Munger House has stood at Cowtown. The house was carefully moved to the museum grounds and restored on site. It was one of the original four buildings of Cowtown and the major building of interest at the museum. The Munger House has seen two major renovations during its time at the museum; the first happened in 1984, and the second occurred in 1998. Through it all, the Munger House has maintained its importance to Cowtown and the city of Wichita.

Chapter One
Darius Munger

Darius Munger was born in Chautauqua County, New York on Aug 21, 1812. He married Julia Phelps in August of 1834. They had their first child, Julia Helen, in 1835 before moving to Chicago.[1]

The Mungers arrived in Manitowoc, Wisconsin on April 17, 1837, where Darius worked as a carpenter and a builder. Darius was also active in local politics, being appointed a road commissioner of District 2 in the county. He served as constable and tax collector and was also a justice of the peace, appointed by the governor in 1848.[2]

In Wisconsin, they bore three more children: Charles Phelps in 1837, Melissa Love in 1840, and Amelia in 1843.

---

[1] J.B. Munger, *The Munger Book* (Chicago: The Tuttle, Morehouse, and Taylor Company, 1915), 301.
[2] Letter of correspondence: Robert P. Fay to Tracie Carr. July 21, 1989. Manitowoc, Wisconsin.

Charles later served in the company E of the 11th Kansas Voluntary Infantry during the Civil War.[3]

The Mungers continued to relocate to different areas. They lived in Ohio in 1848 and 1849. They moved to Missouri in 1850 where they bore their last child Mary Ellen in 1855. They settled in Kansas in 1860, choosing Topeka as their new home.[4]

Seeking a new adventure as a representative of the Wichita Town and Land Company, Darius decided to relocate his family one more time and moved to Wichita in 1868. He began building a home in the fall of 1868 on what is now North Waco Street. His daughter Mary joined him in the spring of 1869, while his wife Julia and his daughter Amelia arrived in Wichita on September 1, 1869.[5]

The home served many functions in early Wichita. They operated one of the city's first hotels, with rooms for rent

---

[3] Munger, 301.
[4] Ibid.
[5] Ibid.; Stan Harder, *D. S. Munger and the Origins of Wichita* (Old Cowtown Museum Archives, 1994), 7.

upstairs. The home also served as a meeting house and judge's chambers. Munger also served as a justice of the peace, beginning in 1868, and post-master while in the home.

While holding the position of justice of the peace, Munger presided over the two-year murder case. Saloon owner M.R. Cordeiro was charged in the death of saloon patron O.J. Whitman; the case was later dismissed.[6]

Munger continued to participate in the development of the area. He signed the petition to organize Sedgwick County, Feb 10, 1870. On March 25, 1870, Munger joined his plat with that of William Greiffenstein at the Butler County Land Office in El Dorado to form the original Wichita town site.[7]

The Munger family kept a nice garden by their home. Note the remarks from *The Wichita City Eagle* on May 23, 1872:

> D. S. Munger led us exultingly through his fine three-acre garden this week and showed us convincing proof of the vegetable productiveness of Arkansas valley soil.

---

[6] H. Craig Miner, *Wichita: The Early Years, 1865-80* (Lincoln, NE: University of Nebraska Press, 1982), 46.

[7] R. M. Long, *Wichita Century* (Wichita, KS: Wichita Historical Museum Association, 1969), 26.

He has been using, for nearly a month, radishes, lettuce and onions gathered in his garden. Gooseberry pie is his latest; and from vines planted last fall in his garden the yield was a quart and a pint to the bush. The prettiest and most enticing place in all the surroundings of this city is the elegantly kept garden of the kind-hearted D.S. We only regret that others who have large grounds do not likewise try to adorn, beautify and turn to practical use so much of God's rich alluvial.[8]

In 1873, Munger acquired the Empire House Hotel at Third and Main. On November 5, 1873 *The Wichita City Eagle* reported: "D. S. Munger, is after a year's rest, at it again, this time in the Empire House, which he has renovated and refitted in such a manner as to call and keep the trade of the traveling public. No kinder, more hospitable, or clever people, live anywhere, than the present host and hostess of the Empire House." In 1874, Munger sold his house to local banker W.C. Woodman. He moved to a small frame house on Water Street.[9]

"Father Munger", as he was affectionately called, continued to be active in the community. Munger began

---

[8] *The Wichita City Eagle*, May 23, 1872. Source found on Newspapers.com; all other newspapers cited found there.
[9] *The Wichita City Eagle*, November 5, 1873.

serving as the coroner starting in 1875. By the end of 1875, Munger took over as keeper of the Daily House at the corner of First and Water; but by December of 1876 he left the hotel industry for good. On April 14, 1879 he was appointed the Police Judge at a rate of $1,000.00 per year and presided over many cases.[10]

Darius Munger passed away in Wichita on December 5, 1879 at the age of 67 after a prolonged illness. His funeral took place at the Episcopal Church and as Marshall Murdock stated, "was attended by the largest number of people ever gathered together upon a funeral occasion in this city," numbering over eight hundred.[11]

---

[10] *The Wichita Weekly Beacon*, Apr 16, 1879.
[11] *The Wichita City Eagle*, Dec 11, 1879.

Darius Munger around the time he arrived in Topeka, Kansas in 1860.

View of Darius Munger around the time he was in Wichita in the 1870s.

Julia Phelps Munger in the 1870s.

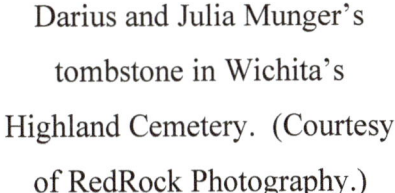

Darius and Julia Munger's tombstone in Wichita's Highland Cemetery. (Courtesy of RedRock Photography.)

Details of Darius (above) and Julia (below) Munger's gravestone in Highland Cemetery.
(Both, courtesy of RedRock Photography.)

Chapter Two
Construction

Darius Munger started building his home in May of 1868 near present day 9th and Waco. He acquired cottonwood logs from Teuchel Island and chopped the logs out with an adze. To join the logs together Munger used lime, sand, and water from the Little Arkansas River along with buffalo hair. Whatever items Munger could not get in Wichita such as windows, doors, and flooring he hauled from Emporia.[12]

Construction was slow at first due to rain as Munger wrote to his friend A. F. Horner in Topeka on May 24, 1868;

> we are getting along very well in preparing timber for building. Although it has been raining nearly half the time during the past week…..It being rainy I had to keep things well covered to secure them from the rain,…we shall have two rooms built ready to occupy in a few days if we have no bad luck….we have already two day boarders and three more wanting to board.[13]

---

[12] "The Story of Wichita's First Dwelling," *The Wichita Daily Eagle,* April 24, 1910.
[13] D. S. Munger to A. F. Horner, May 24, 1868, Horner, A. F., Manuscripts Collection Miscellaneous, Kansas Historical Society.

While constructing the house Munger lived in a tent over what would later become the kitchen section. By the winter of 1868 Munger only had the kitchen section and the first floor of the rest of the house completed.

In March of 1869, the Mungers' youngest child Mary, arrived in Wichita from Topeka, Kansas. She finished a year of schooling at the Episcopal Female Seminary in Topeka. Mary, at the age of 14, helped her father finish the second story, roof, and dormers of the house.[14]

Contrary to local legend and stories of old timers Munger's situation was not as primitive as they would like to report. If he needed certain materials Munger could order them from Topeka or Emporia, and for common everyday items he acquired them from Doctor "Doc" Lewellen's store about 150 feet from his house on North Waco. For the construction of his house, Munger on June 25, 1869 paid $20.00 for 1,000 feet of

---

[14] Harder, 5.; The Episcopal Female Seminary was renamed the College of the Sisters of Bethany in 1873.; A. T., Andreas, *History of the State of Kansas*, (Chicago: A. T. Andreas, 1883), 546.; Tracie Carr, *The Munger Children* located in Old Cowtown Museum Archives, 1988, 1.

lumber to be hauled to 9th and Waco and on June 28, 1869 bought 50 more feet of lumber from Lewellen for $3.00.[15]

On September 1, 1869, Munger's wife, Julia Phelps and daughter, Amelia arrived at the Wichita site. By the fall of 1869 the house was completed and photographed for the first time. The photograph shows a corral to the right of the house and trees along the Little Arkansas River in the background.[16]

---

[15] Doctor Lewellen and John Ward, Ledger "Book A," 1869-1870, Old Cowtown Museum Archives, 20.
[16] Harder, 6-7.

By the winter of 1868, Munger only had the kitchen section and the first floor of the rest of the house completed as shown above. By the fall of 1869, the house was completed and photographed for the first time (below). The photograph shows a corral to the right of the house and trees along the Little Arkansas River in the background.

Page from one of Doctor "Doc" Lewellen's ledgers showing what Darius Munger and his family bought from Lewellen's store from May 2–June 13, 1870.

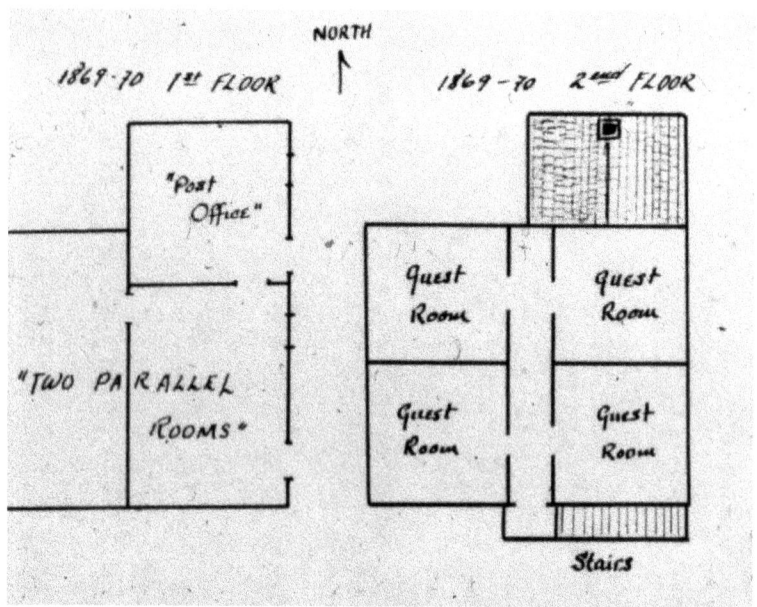

The above image shows the interior layout of the Munger House from 1869-1870. On the left shows the layout of the first story while on the right shows the upper floor layout.

Chapter Three
Munger's Occupation

At the Land Office in Humboldt, Kansas on February 2, 1870, Munger applied for 160 acres in section seventeen of the Wichita Township. He paid $1.25 per acre for a total of $200.00. As witnesses Munger brought along "Doc" Lewellen and James R. Mead. The house, according to Mead, was 20 feet by 24 feet with a shingle roof, 9 doors, and 8 windows. Along with the house Munger also built a sawmill, corral, stables, and a well.[17]

Due to the size of the Munger House, it became the major building for many community offices and activities. The interior of the home had two parallel rooms on the first floor with the one-story kitchen on the north. The front parallel room served as a dining room, hotel lobby, judge's chambers,

---

[17] Applications Submitted to Purchase Land, 1862-1871 No. 230, D. S. Munger, February 2, 1870, Humboldt, Kansas, Land Office; Records of the Bureau of Land Management, Record Group 48; National Archives at Kansas City, Missouri.; Ibid., National Archives Building, Washington, DC.

Munger's office, and as a public meeting place. An outside door in the southeast corner of the room provided direct access to the room for the public. The back parallel room served as the family's bedroom with the Mungers' two daughters, Amelia and Mary Ellen, sleeping on one side and Darius and Julia sleeping on the other with only a sheet for privacy. The kitchen served as a makeshift post office with Munger as postmaster from March 28 to September 27, 1870.[18]

The upstairs housed the hotel rooms that would become the family's primary business. Shortly after the house was completed in 1869 the upstairs became one large room. Early families such as E. B. Allen's, one of Wichita's first physicians, lived in the upstairs of the Munger House. As Allen's young son Charles wrote: "When we first got to Wichita we boarded with old man Munger…we lived up stairs [sic] over the log part of it, and I remember upsetting some water on the floor which was made of cottonwood planks and

---

[18] Neal Danielson, "First Postmasters & Post Offices," http://www.wichitastampclub.org/KPH.html, accessed September 24, 2019.

not very tight and it dripped on old man Munger's bald head and he seriously objected."[19] Along with boarding guests the large room upstairs also held the first service for the Episcopal Church in 1869. The exact date when the upstairs was converted into four rooms is unclear. After its conversion, the upper story had four rooms with a middle hallway and access to the upstairs via an outside staircase.[20]

The hotel business was very profitable for Munger, so much so that in October of 1870 he planned an addition of five additional rooms, two on the first floor and three upstairs. The two additional rooms on the first floor became the hotel office and an addition to the kitchen. Two of the three additional rooms on the second story became guest rooms, with the third being the bride's room. The room was called the bride's room because it always assigned to young married couples. "The

---

[19] Charles C. Allen, *The E. B. Allen Family*, (Wichita, Old Cowtown Museum Archives, n.d.), 2-3.
[20] "One of the Earliest Pioneers Gone," *The Wichita Weekly Beacon,* December 10, 1879.; The Episcopal Church is now known as St. John's Episcopal Church, one of the oldest churches in Wichita.; "Dispute Waxing Warmer," *The Wichita Daily Eagle,* September 10, 1916.

bride's room was just like the rest, only a trifle larger. It had two windows, one looking south and one east."[21]

In 1870, the *Wichita Vidette* proclaimed the quality of the Munger House and the hospitality of the Mungers: "The Munger House…is one of the best kept houses in the State…Mine Host and Hostess of the Munger are known, not only here, but elsewhere for their kindness and general hospitality…For a good meal, superior accommodations, and kind treatment, choose ye, the Munger House, when at Wichita."[22] To keep providing the superior accommodations, the Mungers bought the majority of goods and supplies from Doc Lewellen's store on North Waco. By 1870, the expanding hotel business required many more items from Lewellen's store which ranged from coffee to blankets. In constructing the southern addition in 1870-1871 Munger bought several of the building supplies from Lewellen's store including flooring,

---

[21] "Phase III: Munger House, 1871," Old Cowtown Museum Archives.; Sentence and quote from "Wichita's Oldest Home; Its Latest Residents," *The Wichita Beacon,* September 26, 1926.
[22] *Wichita Vidette,* December 22, 1870.

nails, door locks, and door hinges. By 1871, Lewellen's store continued to supply the majority of Munger's supplies for his hotel and the Munger family. The limited number of supplies bought by Munger in 1872 can be attributed to the growth of North Main Street and the start of the decline of North Waco as the city's commercial center.[23]

In 1873, Munger acquired the Empire House on the northwest corner of 3rd and North Main Streets. A year later he sold the old log Munger House on North Waco to W. C. Woodman, a local banker. Thus, ends Munger's involvement with one of Wichita's first homes.

---

[23] Doctor Lewellen and John Ward, Ledger Books "A-C," 1869-1870, Old Cowtown Museum Archives.; A full list of building supplies for the 1871 addition is included in the appendix.; The 1871 items are listed in Ledgers "A"& "B".

Due to the family's growing hotel business Darius Munger added four rooms (one on the first floor and three on the second) and an addition to the Kitchen section in 1870.

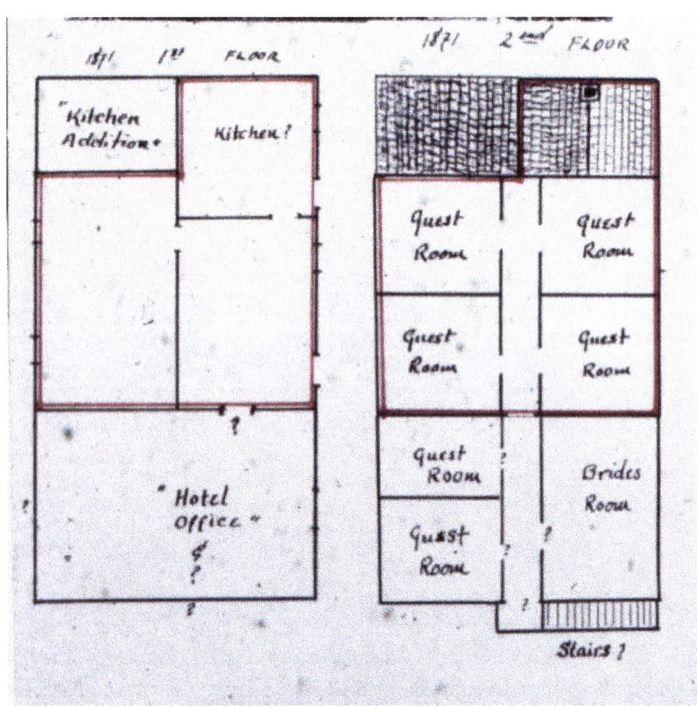

Chapter Four
Woodman's Occupation

On June 10, 1874, W. C. Woodman, a local banker, acquired the Munger House and property from Darius Munger. The date of the acquisition occurred on the 11th wedding anniversary of W. C. and Elizabeth Woodman. A year later he moved the house one block south to present day 8th and Waco and built a mansion around it called "Lakeside."[24]

In 1948, Rea Woodman, W. C. Woodman's daughter, described in great detail the plants and trees that adorned the grounds Lakeside was on. She wrote:

> With the house, he bought a large acreage, marging [sic] the Little River. As I remember it all there was a large pasture on the extreme north; an orchard of bearing apple trees; a large vineyard of Concord and Delaware grapes; a south lawn, at first just beautiful prairie in which father spent all his leisure planting trees, a long narrow, boxed-in flower garden just north of the house; a woodpile; and a big kitchen garden. There were six big, cherry trees back of the barn…And two such handsome apricot trees east of the barn, with a roadway winding between them. The barn was of log, a structure in make and finish the

---

[24] *Memorandum of Interview with Miss Woodman about Munger House,* Richard M. Long Papers, Kansas Historical Society, 1.

counterpart of the house. The house and barn were on a line, the barn was between the house and river and the dog kennel were east of the barn…Next to the orchard, toward the river, was a group of thriving cottonwoods that we called The Grove…and east of The Grove, nearer the river, in a beautiful hollow where wood violets and Christmas berry bushes grew…There was a long grape arbor between the house and the orchard…Between the house and the woodhouse…stood an enormous drooping bunch of greenery called "Washington Willow."[25]

Darius Munger planted all the trees and plants when he owned the land from 1868-1874.[26]

When building Lakeside in 1875 Woodman greatly changed the interior of the original Munger House. In the original house the downstairs contained two parallel rooms going north to south. Munger used the front room as a bar and the back room where customers ate. During the transformation into Lakeside, the bar room was converted into Woodman's study. Woodman also added a large parlor and two additional bedrooms above it on the south side of the house. He then added a grand Victorian tower above the one-story kitchen part

---

[25] H. Rea Woodman, *Wichitana, 1877-1897* (Wichita: H. Rea Woodman, 1948), 22-23.
[26] Ibid., 24.

of the Munger House and made an addition to the rear of the tower which housed Lakeside's kitchen and dining room. During this remodel Woodman added an interior staircase in either in the tower portion or in the kitchen/dining room addition.[27]

Once completed, Lakeside was one of the most fashionable buildings built in Wichita and one of fifteen drawings located in the Centennial Issue of *The Wichita Eagle* in 1876. *The Eagle* wrote:

> Delightfully and picturesquely situated, near the norther limits of the city, on the elevated banks of the lake formed by the Little Arkansas River, with a back-ground of tall cottonwood trees, upon the very spot where the Wichita warrior was wont [sic] to pitch his wigwam, and close beside the magnificent old elm, under the dense shadow of whose spreading branches for generations the peace calumet passed from mouth to mouth in the solemn council of the now departed braves, stands the residence of W. C. Woodman.[28]

---

[27] *Memorandum of Interview with Miss Woodman About Munger House*, 3. The interior staircase is fondly remembered by older guests. After its move to Old Cowtown Museum in 1952 the stairs were used by visitors as access to the second story. In 1984, the restoration of the house to its 1869-1871 version forced the removal of the interior stairs.

[28] "Lakeside,' The Residence of W. C. Woodman," *The Wichita Eagle*, April 6, 1876.

W. C. Woodman lived in Lakeside until his death in 1887. By December 6, 1896, only Elizabeth, Woodman's wife, and Rea, Woodman's daughter, lived in Lakeside. Less than a month later Elizabeth and Rea left Wichita. Elizabeth went to Chicago, Illinois and Rea went to Lawrence to work on her Master's degree at the University of Kansas.[29] "Wichita was a memory," wrote Rea Woodman. "Our faces were set toward new things. Eastward Ho!"[30] Thus, ended the second part of the Munger House story.

W. C. Woodman in 1863, eleven years before his purchase of the Munger House.

---

[29] "Death of W. C. Woodman-In Memoriam," *The Wichita Eagle,* December 27, 1887.; Woodman, 280.; "Among the Ladies," *The Wichita Daily Eagle,* December 6, 1886.; Woodman, 282.
[30] Woodman, 282.

On June 10, 1874, W. C. Woodman, a local banker, acquired the Munger House and property from Darius Munger. A year later he moved the house one block south to present day 8th and Waco and built a mansion around it called "Lakeside."

When building Lakeside in 1875, Woodman greatly changed the interior of the original Munger House. He also added a parlor seen above, c.1889; and a library seen below, c.1889. (Both, courtesy of the Rea Woodman Collection at the McCormick School Museum.)

Chapter Five
Other Owners

The Woodman family continued to live in Lakeside after the death of their patriarch. But after a tax default by the Woodmans, the Lakeside mansion was purchased P.J. Conklin in 1897.[31] Mr. Conklin moved into the home with his wife and family.

In 1901, major damage affected the house. On the upper story a fire broke out within the newly installed chimney. While everyone was safe, the top floor was "badly scorched and burned" with the south part of the roof almost entirely burned up. The fire caused approximately $500.00 worth of damage.[32]

After the damage, the Conklins fixed the home and updated it to their liking. The private bedrooms upstairs were

---
[31] Katie Shewmake, "Munger House...history captured in 4 walls," *The Wichita Eagle and Beacon,* Aug 31, 1975.
[32] "First Hotel in Wichita," *The Wichita Eagle,* November 29, 1901.

remodeled after the fire, and the roof was replaced. The public area on the main floor consisted of a living room, kitchen, library, and a dining room to seat at least twenty. Siding was also added to the exterior.[33]

Mrs. Conklin was very active in Wichita society and hosted many gatherings at her home. Many church socials congregated here. There were picnics for the Hypatia Club and the Sunflower Chatauqua Ladies outside of the home. Also, Mrs. Conklin hosted receptions for Fairmount College students.[34]

One specific gathering of note occurred in 1902. The Conklins hosted a Fourth of July celebration at their home, inviting many local families to enjoy the holiday. One guest of importance was reigning Governor of Kansas William Stanley. Governor Stanley even delivered an impassioned address about trees.[35]

---

[33] *The Wichita Daily Eagle*, Apr 8, 1909.
[34] *The Wichita Daily Eagle*, July 5, 1902.
[35] Ibid.

And in 1909, with many Wichita citizens present for the special day, Mr. and Mrs. Conklin's daughter Julia was married in the home.

The Conklins began listing their house for sale as early as 1908. The local Daughters of the American Revolution were interested in purchasing the home, due to its historic origination.[36]

In 1910, there was a city-wide controversy surrounding the former Munger House. P.J. Conklin donated a small cabin to the city that was then restored in Riverside Park; Conklin claimed it was part of the old Munger House. Mr. Munger's daughter, Mary Munger Watson, disputed the claim; she was 14 years old when the house was built and resided in it. In addition, Fred A. Sowers, a local pioneer and founder of the *Wichita Vidette* and *The Wichita Beacon*, claimed that the restored cabin was none other than the old saloon of one John

---

[36] "Would Preserve Old House," *The Wichita Daily Eagle,* May 19, 1908.

Gifford. It was finally decided that the Riverside Park cabin was not the former Munger House.[37]

Dr. John and Emiline Fuller eventually purchased the land and house from the Conklins in October of 1911. They used Wichita realtor Bert Howard. The couple had previously lived at 17th and Minnie Avenue in Wichita.[38]

After purchasing the home and finding out its history as the old Munger place, Dr. Fuller mentioned how numerous people asked him for relics of the house, such as small pieces of the outer logs. Dr. Fuller told the newspaper we would always deny them.[39]

The Fullers decided to relocate the house west in late 1911, and had it moved several hundred feet in that direction. The new address became 920 Back Bay Boulevard. During the

---

[37] "Cabin was Border Day Saloon Not Old Munger Home," *The Wichita Eagle*, April 27, 1910.
[38] "A New Flat is Planned," *The Wichita Beacon*, October 14, 1911.
[39] Ibid.

move the house stayed intact, with only plaster cracking in one place.[40]

The home maintained its charm. It still had original glass from Munger, as of 1926. It was also the warmest house in the winter and coolest house in the summer, due to great insulation.[41]

However, the Fullers did make some changes. They had a bathroom installed on the second floor. The house was wired for electricity; previously it had side lights with exposed wiring. They enlarged the kitchen and extended the second story over the kitchen. The owners added porches and the house was heated by stoves through flues in the kitchen.[42]

After occupying the home for three decades, the Fullers sold the home to Mrs. Robert Foulston in 1942.

The local Eunice Sterling Chapter of the Daughters of the American Revolution had been interested in purchasing the

---

[40] Bliss Isley, "Wichita's Oldest Home: Its Latest Resident," *The Wichita Beacon*, September 26, 1926.
[41] Ibid.
[42] Ibid.

old Munger House for decades. As first reported in 1908 by the local newspaper, when Conklin put the home on the market, the organization became interested. They stated that Wichita had been tearing down old buildings for years without much forethought as to their importance, and it was up to the D.A.R. to keep some buildings from destruction. Even though Conklin's initial asking price of $8,500.00 was too much for the organization at that time, they never gave up hope.[43]

In 1942, the old Munger House again became available. While the asking price was $3,000.00, it also came with an estimated $7,000.00 worth of needed restorations. The Daughters of the American Revolution finally purchased the building that year with the help of Juanita Foulston.[44]

Restorations began quickly. With less than $2,000.00 initially, the D.A.R. started restorations, beginning with the

---

[43] "Would Preserve Old House," *The Wichita Daily Eagle,* May 19, 1908.

[44] "Darius Sales Munger House," National Register of Historic Places Nomination Form, (Washington, DC: U.S. Department of the Interior, National Park Service, 2013), 5.; Blanche D. Oliver, *Historical Sketch of Munger House* (Old Cowtown Museum Archives, 1961), 2.

removal of all non-original additions to the house. After years of fundraising and little progress made on the house, the D.A.R decided to find the Munger House a new home. They got in touch with the newly formed Historic Wichita Inc. According to Historic Wichita board member Dick Long, the D.A.R offered Historic Wichita the Munger House, a lot worth $1,500.00, plus $3,000.00 to have the home restored and moved to their property. In October of 1951, the D.A.R. presented the deed to the house to Historic Wichita Inc. The new acquisition was then moved to Cowtown in 1952 and work began. In total the cost of restoration eclipsed $16,000.00.[45]

---

[45] *Notes on the Munger House*, Old Cowtown Museum Archives, 2.; "Historic Wichita Acquires House," *The Wichita Eagle*, October 6, 1951.; "Munger House Gets Attention," *Wichita Cow Town Vidette*, March 30, 1961.

Riverside Park cabin, once claimed as the old Munger House. c. 1910.

FOR SALE

901 Waco St.   150 Feet Frontage

From 400 to 600 feet back to river. 12-room modern house, barn, chicken houses, etc. Plenty of fruit, very cheap at $11,000 $5000. cash will swing it.

61 feet laying immediately south of the above property. One of the best residence locations in Wichita.

Price $3500.00

Inquire of P. J. Conklin Loan Co.

Both Phones 624   107 S. Main

1908 advertisement by P. J. Conklin for his house at 901 North Waco. His home included the old Munger House.
(Courtesy of *The Wichita Eagle*.)

1926 view of the Fuller residence at 920 Back Bay Boulevard with some of the Woodman's additions. The original Munger log house is to the right of the bay window.
(Courtesy of *The Wichita Beacon*.)

In the hands of the Eunice Sterling Chapter of the Daughters of the American Revolution the old Munger House sat vacant at 920 Back Bay Boulevard with the upper photograph dated to 1945 and the bottom photograph dated to 1947.

Chapter Six
Munger House at Cowtown

A year after the Eunice Sterling Chapter of the Daughters of the American Revolution donated the deed to the Munger House to Historic Wichita, Inc., the house was on the move to a 23 acre site on the north bank of the Big Arkansas River in 1952. The D. E. Tandy Company moved the house to its new location. It was fitting that Tandy was chosen to move the house in August of 1952 since he helped move the house in 1912 from 8th and Waco to Back Bay Boulevard.[46] According to Tandy "it's a lot easier to move now than it was in 1912. We raised it up on hand turned jacks and pulled it with a team of horses. Today we just put some hydraulic jacks under the house, backed a trailer under it and we can drive it away behind a truck."[47]

---

[46] "Pioneer House will be Moved," *The Wichita Eagle,* August 8, 1952.;
[47] "Historic Residence Being Moved to Site in Cow-town," *The Wichita Eagle,* August 19, 1952.

Once the Munger House arrived at Cowtown minus its second story, it was orientated east-west instead of its original north-south orientation. Members of Historic Wichita, Inc. restored the house as close to its original condition by using the same methods that Munger used in 1868-1869. They added Cottonwood logs from the banks of the Arkansas River to the original 1860s logs, with much of the old plaster ground up and used in the new plaster. In the restored upstairs, Cowtown founders preserved two sections of the plaster and willow lath used in the original construction of the house. These renovations brought the house back to its 1868-1869 version, which contained 3 rooms downstairs (2 parallel rooms and a kitchen) and 4 upstairs. By 1953, the restoration was completed with the finished house being used as the backdrop for a square dance photo.[48]

---

[48] "Munger's Methods will be Used in Restoring House for Cow Town of 1872," *The Wichita Eagle*, October 10, 1952.; The Munger House is one of the first four buildings moved to what would become Old Cowtown Museum in 1952. The other three are the First Presbyterian Church, Hodge House, and the Jail.

Over the years the interior of the house changed with one thing remaining consistent: the furnishings have no connection to the Munger family but are of the 1870s to 1880s. The restored interior kept the interior stairs off the kitchen that led to the four rooms on the second story; Woodman installed these when he added on to the house in 1874. From the 1950s until 1984, the front parallel room was interpreted as a parlor/sitting room and later a dining room. Cowtown staff interpreted the back parallel room as a family room from the 1950s until the 1984 restoration. The upstairs of the house originally at Cowtown had four unequal rooms due to the interior staircase. The 1984 restoration made all four of the upstairs rooms equal, eliminated the interior staircase, and added an exterior staircase to the westside of the house.

Throughout the years the Munger House had been a popular place for pictures, including ones of square dances and pow-wows. The house has also become a mecca for Munger's relatives. On October 28, 1961, Edgard A. Williams, great-grandson of Darius Munger, and his family visited Cowtown and saw the Munger House. The Williamses were impressed with the house, with Edgar's son, Richard, saying "It's a pretty neat house. But it must have been pretty hard then without television."[49]

On June 14, 1982, the Munger House was added to the National Register of Historic Places. It was the 16th building in Wichita added to the register. Its listing gave provenance to the house and helped start fundraising efforts to restore it in 1984.[50]

---

[49] Sentence and quote from "Lowell Thomas Travel Key Includes Wichita Cow Town," *The Wichita Eagle*, April 20, 1961.
[50] U.S. Department of the Interior, National Park Service, "National Register Database," https://www.nps.gov/subjects/national register/upload/national_register_listed_20190404_withlinks.xlsx, accessed September 27, 2019.

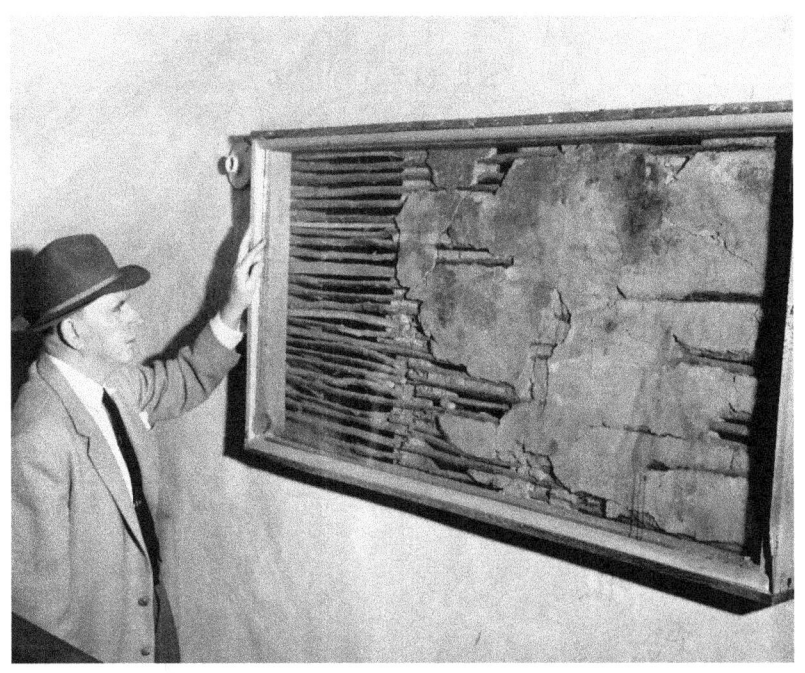

Above, Richard "Dick" Long is showing one of the two preserved sections of the plaster and willow lath used in the original construction of the house that Cowtown founders saved in the restored upstairs.

With the renovations complete the house became a backdrop for many events and promotional shots such as square dances.

By the end of 1955 Cowtown grew from 4 buildings to 10 buildings. This view looking to the west shows the Munger House in the foreground with the old Cow Town Fire Station No. 1 in the left background.

In 1958 Munger's granddaughter, Mable Watson Foley came to Cowtown and posed in front of the Munger House.

Along with Mable Watson Foley, Mable Foley Randall, Munger's great-grand-daughter (left) and Jolenn Randall, Munger's great-great-grand-daughter posing in front of the Munger House in 1958.

Over the years the Munger House has been used as a backdrop for many promotional photographs including the Hon-Pe-Aika Indian Dancers in 1963 and the regional radio station KFDI in the 1960s showing their "Stage Coach" mobile unit. (Below image, courtesy author.)

From the 1950s to 1984, the front parallel room (below) was interpreted as a parlor/sitting room and later a dining room. Cowtown staff interpreted the back parallel room (left) as a family room from the 1950s until the 1984 restoration.

The 1950s restored interior kept the interior stairs off the kitchen (left) that led to the four rooms on the second story. The keeping of the interior stairs resulted into a smaller kitchen section (below) than the original house had in the 1870s.

Due to the interior staircase the upstairs of the house originally at Cowtown had four unequal rooms with a hallway to each room.

The upstairs of the house originally at Cowtown was decorated with "period" furnishings. In 1984, the rooms were redone to 1870 accounts of the second story and became vacant.

Chapter Seven
Restorations

In the early 1980s, Historic Wichita began research and preparation to restore the Munger House. After years of being exposed to the elements, the house needed additional care to maintain its structure and appeal. Thus, began a three-year process of work determining the right course of action.[51]

To restore the Munger House to its original floor plan, the board of directors relied heavily on the notes of Mary Munger. There were three main changes made to the Munger House during this restoration. First, the inner staircase was moved to the outside which coincided with how the original house had access to the upstairs for those seeking hotel accommodations; it was added after W.C. Woodman purchased the home in 1874. Secondly, the top floor was converted back to four rooms from three, as per the Mary Munger letters. And

---

[51] Kansas Preservation newsletter. (July-August 1984, Vol VI, No. 5).

finally, new walnut logs were added to the foundation to reinforce the stability of the structure's foundation[52].

In order to make these changes, the board of directors needed to raise the money. When all was said and done, they raised $84,665.00 The amount came from three different areas. First, $30,759.00 came from a community development block grant money from the City of Wichita. Second, $26,953.00 of the money saw the National Park Service distribute the funds via the Department of Historic Preservation part of the Kansas State Historical Society. The remaining $26,953.00 came from private donations; some of the larger donors included money from the Weideman Foundation's corporate fund drive, and the Wichita Area Board of Realtors[53].

Once the necessary funds were raised, Historic Wichita Inc. began hiring specialists for the project. The museum used Construction & Management Inc. and Wildcat Construction Co. as the general contractors. Watson, Briedenthal, Burk, and

---

[52] Seth Effron, "$84,665 Set to Restore Munger House," *The Wichita Eagle-Beacon*, June 15, 1983.
[53] Ibid.

Associates of Wichita were hired as the architects. And finally, a Maryland preservation consultant named Douglass Reed, from Preservation Associates, helped with both research and physical restoration[54].

Once the project was complete, the following work had been performed. They lifted the roof to its original height. The three rooms upstairs were recreated to four guest rooms. They built an outside staircase. The foundation was raised about 1.5 feet and put on a limestone block base. Beams were placed under the house and jacks and pilings were installed at the corners. The builders also replaced walnut and cottonwood logs, along with damaged plaster and cement daubings.[55]

By 1987, the Munger House needed more restorations and updates. This second restoration, known as the Munger House Research and Restoration Project, projected a cost of

---

[54] *The Munger House at Old Cowtown Museum.* (Old Cowtown Museum: 1984), 1,9.

[55] Ellen Schechet, "Craftsmen Turn Back Clock at Munger House," *The Wichita Eagle-Beacon,* March 3, 1984.

$21,000.00. The goal of the project focused on making the first-floor interior more historically accurate.

The money funded many areas. First, work started in March to replicate the original Munger House floor; with a ¼" subfloor, the new floor would be laid north to south as noted by Munger relatives and be of fine finish. Next, new plaster work sealed up the house and walls. In April, baseboards and door and window trim board were installed. Finally, the staff exhibit preparations team painted the new woodwork while also preparing the first-floor rooms for exhibit setup.[56]

Funding and research was done by the Junior League of Wichita. They focused on early area newspapers to verify information. The Junior League donated $12,500.00 for the project. Provided in three installments these payments went towards each phase. For example, Jerry G. Rogers Lathing and Plastering Company invoiced a cost of $4,260.00 for plastering walls and ceilings, plastering the chimney, as well as plastering

---

[56] Stan Harder, *Curatorial Department Annual Report*, Old Cowtown Museum Archives, 1987.

the two west rooms. Also, $150.00 was used to purchase two brass reproduction lights for the downstairs rooms[57]

The restorations were complete in time for an unveiling at the Old Sedgwick County Fair event in the fall. These renovations gave the Munger House the structural and visual improvements necessary to better portray the early life of the family.

After ten years of observing the changing conditions, Old Cowtown Museum decided it was again time to have another restoration of the Munger House. Water had again damaged some of the logs on the house and needed replacing. Better sealing was necessary. But with the cost of another renovation looming, the Cowtown Board of Directors decided to try it a different way.

It was agreed upon that to save costs, staff and volunteers trained by a proper preservationist would complete the repairs. The proposal of Conservation Services from

---

[57] Suzie Ahlstrand to Elizabeth Kennedy, Junior League of Wichita letter, July 18, 1986.

Pueblo, Colorado was selected to coordinate this type of workshop. Working with the architecture firm William Morris Associates, tasks taught and supervised by Conservation Services and their supervisor Harrison Goodall included epoxy stabilization, preservative and water repellents, and log treatments. All the materials were provided by Cowtown, including squared and seasoned logs, epoxies, preservatives, and repellents.[58]

Beginning in October, the group went to work. About a dozen staff and volunteers of Cowtown helped in this effort. Costs incurred during this projected totaled about $15,000.00.[59] These repairs helped complete the mission of restoring Munger to its original glory and fulfilled the thoughts of the D.A.R. when they first acquired the house:

---

[58] Conservation Services proposal of 1998.
[59] Becky Tanner, "Historic Munger house in Cowtown is receiving a face-lift," *The Wichita Eagle*, November 2, 1998.

"This first home is not a mere pile of wood and cement. It is a symbol of, and a monument to the efforts of the pioneers of Wichita. It speaks more forcefully than words, of the struggle for existence, of the courage and accomplishments of our pioneers."[60]

---

[60] *Notes on the Munger House*, 2.

After years of being exposed to the elements, the house needed additional care to maintain its structure and appeal (above). In 1984, restoration of the structure replaced logs especially in the Kitchen section (below).

The 1984 restoration included the removal of cottonwood logs from the kitchen section that were added during the 1950s restoration. To replace the 1950s ones, replacement logs were made using the same techniques that Darius Munger did in 1868.

During the restoration workers built an outside staircase (below). The foundation was raised about 1.5 feet and put on a limestone block base (above). Beams were placed under the house and jacks and pilings were installed at the corners.

In 1987, the Munger House got new floors replicated like Munger's original floors in all of the first-floor rooms including the Front Room, as seen as above.

Ten years later another restoration of the Munger House was completed due to poor sealant between the logs.

Conclusion

Darius Munger was an important figure in the history of Wichita for many reasons. He contributed to the Wichita Town and Land Company which helped settle the area. He served as a post-master, justice of the peace, and hotel entrepreneur. He built one of the first houses in Wichita, known as the Munger House.

Munger built his house using his bare hands during the fall of 1868 and the spring of 1869. He used local cottonwood logs and purchased tools from "Doc" Lewellen's store. Other items he needed were shipped down from Emporia. His daughter Mary helped put the finishing touches on the house. It was later expanded in 1870.

The Munger House stands as a tribute to Wichita. Its construction mirrors that of the city. By 1872, both were prominent places in the area. Early Wichita looked at the Munger House as a staple to promote the area to possible settlers and businesses.

The Munger House tells the early history of Wichita. Born upon the riverbanks, both appeared from nothing to give the western settler a place to stay and a place to call home. Both expanded as necessary to facilitate a growing population.

While most early homes and buildings have long since passed through time, the Munger House lives on. It symbolizes that early settler spirit on the Arkansas River. The house never surrendered to the odds. Like Wichita, the survival of the Munger House continues to give the new generation hope for the future.

Bibliography

Books

Andreas, A. T., History of the State of Kansas. Chicago: A. T. Andreas, 1883.

Long, Richard M. Wichita Century: A Pictorial History of Wichita, Kansas 1870-1970. Wichita: Wichita Historical Museum Association, 1969.

Miner, H. Craig. Wichita: The Early Years, 1865-80. Lincoln, NE: University of Nebraska Press, 1982.

Munger, J. B. The Munger Book. Chicago: The Tuttle, Morehouse, and Taylor Company, 1915.

Woodman, H. Rea. Wichitana, 1877-1897. Wichita: H. Rea Woodman, 1948.

Manuscripts

Allen, Charles C. The E. B. Allen Family. Wichita: n.p., n.d. Old Cowtown Museum Archives.

Applications Submitted to Purchase Land, 1862-1871, No.230, D. S. Munger, February 2, 1870, Humboldt, Kansas, Land Office; Records of the Bureau of Land Management, Record Group 48; National Archives at Kansas City, Missouri.; Ibid., National Archives Building, Washington, DC.

Carr, Tracie. The Munger Children. Wichita: Old Cowtown Museum, 1988. Old Cowtown Museum Archives.

D. S. Munger to A. F. Horner, May 24, 1868, Horner, A. F., Manuscripts Collection Miscellaneous, Kansas Historical Society.

"Darius Sales Munger House," National Register of Historic Places Nomination Form Draft. Washington, DC: U.S. Department of the Interior, National Park Service, 1982. Old Cowtown Museum Building Files.

Doctor Lewellen and John Ward, Ledger Books "A-D." Wichita: Doctor Lewellen and John Ward, 1868-1873. Old Cowtown Museum Archives.

Harder, Stan. Curatorial Department Annual Report. Wichita: Old Cowtown Museum, 1987. Old Cowtown Museum Archives.

----------------. D. S. Munger and the Origins of Wichita. Wichita: Old Cowtown Museum, 1994. Old Cowtown Museum Archives.

--------------. *The Munger House 1868-1874,* Old Cowtown Museum Archives.

Letter of correspondence: Robert P. Fay to Tracie Carr. July 21, 1989. Manitowoc, Wisconsin. Old Cowtown Museum Building Files.

Memorandum of Interview with Miss Woodman about Munger House, Richard M. Long Papers, Kansas Historical Society.

The Munger House at Old Cowtown Museum. Wichita: Old Cowtown Museum, 1984. Old Cowtown Museum Archives.

Notes on the Munger House. Wichita: n.p. n.d. Old Cowtown Museum Archives.

Oliver, Blanche D. Historical Sketch of Munger House. Wichita: Old Cowtown Museum, 1961. Old Cowtown Museum Archives, 1961.

Phase III: Munger House, 1871. Old Cowtown Museum Archives.

Suzie Ahlstrand to Elizabeth Kennedy, Junior League of Wichita letter, July 18, 1986. Old Cowtown Museum Building Files.

Newspapers
The Daily Beacon (Wichita, Kansas)

The Wichita Beacon (Wichita, Kansas)

The Wichita City Eagle (Wichita, Kansas)

Wichita Cow Town Vidette (Wichita, Kansas)

The Wichita Daily Eagle (Wichita, Kansas)

The Wichita Eagle (Wichita, Kansas)

The Wichita Eagle and Beacon (Wichita, Kansas)

Wichita Vidette (Wichita, Kansas)

The Wichita Weekly Beacon (Wichita, Kansas)

Websites

Danielson, Neal. "First Postmasters & Post Offices,"
 http://www.wichitastampclub.org/KPH.html.
 Accessed September 24, 2019.

U.S. Department of the Interior, National Park Service,
 "National Register Database," https://www.nps.gov/
 subjects/nationalregister/upload/national_register_
 listed_20190404_withlinks.xlsx.
 Accessed September 27, 2019.

Appendix

Present day view of the Munger House exterior
(Courtesy of Keith Wondra.)

Present day views of the Munger House showing the kitchen (above) and the front room (below). (Above courtesy of Crystal Socha, and below courtesy of Keith Wondra.)

Present day views of the Munger House bedrooms
(Both, courtesy of Crystal Socha.)

In 1983, local historic preservationists placed a metal marker (left) near the original location of the Munger House at 9th and Waco Streets. (Courtesy of Keith Wondra.)

In 2019, due to theft a stone plaque replaced the metal sign. (Courtesy of Crystal Socha.)

www.ingramcontent.com/pod-product-compliance
Lightning Source LLC
Chambersburg PA
CBHW071121160426
43196CB00013B/2667